Anonymous

Fort Payne, Alabama

Vol. 1

Anonymous

Fort Payne, Alabama
Vol. 1

ISBN/EAN: 9783337713720

Printed in Europe, USA, Canada, Australia, Japan

Cover: Foto ©ninafisch / pixelio.de

More available books at **www.hansebooks.com**

FORT PAYNE, ALABAMA,

ILLUSTRATED.

February, 1889 --- August, 1890.

PUBLISHED BY THE

Fort Payne Coal and Iron Company,

CAPITAL, $5,000,000.

"It is the intention of the stockholders and officers of The Fort Payne Coal and Iron Company to build a manufacturing city in the Wills Valley at Fort Payne, and if the results obtained in other localities, many of them with far less advantages, can be taken as a criterion, the accomplishment of the object can readily be attained. The Company has laid the foundations broad, and surrounded the enterprise with men whose financial skill and judgment are a guarantee that the inexhaustible resources of this fine property will be carefully and fully developed, and, as a natural result of such development, a city will rise in its midst."—[Prospectus, January, 1889.

FOR THE FULFILMENT OF THE PROMISES QUOTED ABOVE, THE READER IS REFERRED TO THE FOLLOWING PAGES.

JOURNAL PRINTING HOUSE, ELIZABETH, N. J.
1890.

OFFICERS.

President,	COL. J. W. SPAULDING.
First Vice-President,	HON. D. H. GOODELL.
Second Vice-President,	HON. HENRY B. PEIRCE.
Manager,	HON. C. O. GODFREY.
Treasurer,	F. H. TOBEY, Fort Payne, Alabama.
Secretary,	HENRY T. POPE, Fort Payne, Alabama.

BOARD OF DIRECTORS.

W. P. RICE, Fort Payne, President Union Investment Co., Kansas City.

HON. D. H. GOODELL, Governor of New Hampshire, Antrim, N. H.

HON. HENRY B. PEIRCE, Secretary of State of Massachusetts, Abington, Massachusetts.

GEN. SELDEN CONNOR, ex-Governor of Maine, President of Northern Banking Company, Portland, Maine.

COL. J. W. SPAULDING, Fort Payne, Alabama.

HON. F. G. JILLSON, Vice-President and Treasurer of Rhode Island Mortgage and Trust Co., Providence, Rhode Island.

HORATIO ADAMS, Kingston, Massachusetts.

DR. J. M. FORD, Kansas City, Missouri.

C. O. GODFREY, ex-Mayor of Fort Payne, Alabama.

GENERAL OFFICES:
FORT PAYNE, ALABAMA.

BRANCH OFFICES:
15 STATE STREET, BOSTON, MASS.
403 PROVIDENT BLD'G, PHILA., PA.

The Fort Payne Coal and Iron Company.

. . . .

THE Fort Payne Coal and Iron Company was organized in the fall of 1888, and after making a close examination of mineral lands in Alabama, purchased thirty-two thousand acres of land in the vicinity of Fort Payne, DeKalb County.

The site of the city in January, 1889, was a little village on the Alabama Great Southern Railroad, fifty-one miles south from Chattanooga, Tenn., and ninety-one miles north from Birmingham.

At a meeting held in Birmingham in November, 1888, the organization was completed, officers and directors elected, and the capital of the company fixed at five million dollars. Four million dollars of the stock was afterwards offered to the public, mainly in the New England states, and was taken in one month. Ten thousand shares were reserved as treasury stock, and was offered to the original stockholders a few months ago ; it was readily taken by them and their friends.

On the fourth of February, 1889, the pioneers of the new city arrived in the town, and began the foundations of a community that has grown with such rapidity and solidity that it astonishes even its most sanguine advocates. The work of surveying, grading and building has gone on steadily until now—about eighteen months since it began—a model city stands on the cotton fields in the Wills Valley.

The camera of the photographer, which always tells the truth, exhibits in the pages of this book the results of the untiring energy and sleepless care of the projectors and directors of this enterprise. The city, however, changes daily, and by the time this book reaches its readers many new features not portrayed will be fixtures in Fort Payne.

Those who first visited this valley were charmed with its beauty and were loud in its praises, and a closer acquaintance has proved that the city and surrounding country reveals new beauties of scenery every time they are visited.

FORT PAYNE IN 1888.

The mountain ranges—Lookout on the east and Sand Mountain on the west—are delightful, winter and summer ; they abound in romantic scenery, rocky glens and tumbling water. Within twenty miles there are untrodden forests and dense jungles where wild beasts and game abound. The location, from 800 to 1200 feet above tide water, tempers the sun's heat even on the hottest days, and the nights are cool and restful. The water that supplies the city is drawn from springs fed by the streams that flow from the heart of the mountain.

The men who control Fort Payne are mainly from New England. Many of the most energetic citizens, however, are either natives of the county or young men from various southern cities.

The greatest care has been taken in the description in this book of the mineral resources of the Company, to show exactly what have been developed by the experts and engineers employed. The results of the work for the past eighteen months are detailed by them in the articles on iron and coal, etc.

The mining and manufacture of iron being one of the chief industries of Fort Payne, the Coal and Iron Company have made extra efforts to encourage the establishment of iron-working plants, and in a short time the raw material will be introduced at the southern end of the city at the furnaces, and from thence pass to the Alabama Hardware Manufacturing Company and other factories at the northern part of the city, and be put on the market as finished goods.

One of the principal plants built by the company is the Fire Brick and Tile works. It is one of the largest and best appointed works in the United States, and now manufactures fire brick and tiles, drain and sewer pipe, and terra cotta work. It is now pushed

MAINE STREET, FORT PAYNE.

Much yet remains to be done to fully develop the great deposits of coal and iron, but what has been accomplished has been done thoroughly and with a view to the future. Selections have been made of various scenes and buildings to give an idea of the progress of the works of the Coal and Iron Company, but it would be impossible in the limits of this work to portray all that could be shown.

to the fullest capacity, and will be enlarged shortly in order to meet demands for its wares, both in Fort Payne and elsewhere.

A complete stove works, making nearly 100 patterns of stoves and varieties of hollow ware, has already become crowded for room, and must immediately increase its capacity in order to supply stoves, etc., ordered from various parts of the South and West. The plant belongs to the Company.

General Offices Fort Payne Coal and Iron Company.

The elaborate system of water works which supplies water to the city has now nine miles of mains and fifty fire-plugs in the corporation limits, and furnishes pure, sparkling water, of which the following analysis was made by Prof. Leffman, of Philadelphia, April 29th, 1890:

715 WALNUT ST.,
PHILADELPHIA,
Apr. 29, 1890.

Dear Sir:

The following are the results of the analysis of the sample of water sent by you. The figures are in grains to the U. S. gallon:

Total Solids, . . 7.14
Chlorine, . . .26
Sul in Sulphates, .15
Calcium, . . 7.64
Magnesium, . .11
Nitrogen in Nitrites, . . . NONE
Nitrogen in Nitrate, ...02
Nitrogen in Ammonium, . NONE
Nitrogen by Permanganate, .0043

The above results indicated water of high organic purity. The total solids consist almost entirely of calcium carbonate. The quantity of this is calculated from the calcium amounting to 6.5 grains per U. S. gallon. The water is quite suitable for all manufacturing purposes. It is an excellent drinking water.

HENRY LEFFMAN.

An electric light plant furnishes arc lights for street purposes and incandescent lights for stores, public buildings and dwellings, and is the property of the parent company.

The DeKalb Hotel, erected by the Company in 1889, upon an entire square in the centre of the city, at a large cost, is modern and complete in all its appointments, and ranks among the best hotels in the Union. It has been patronized by thousands and has merited the warm encomiums passed upon it by guests from home and abroad. It has made the stay of visitors from the North to Fort Payne pleasant and agreeable, and is a favorite resort of the entire country within 100 miles, on account of its cuisine and admirable management.

Early in the formation of the city an exhibit hall was built by the managers in which to show the various ores, coals, timbers, clays, etc., to be found on the property of the Company. This hall has become entirely inadequate to contain the various specimens, etc., and a new and elegant building in which to display not only ores, but all manufactures of iron, wood, clay, etc., produced in the city, will be built opposite the new railway station.

One of the natural curiosities of Fort Payne is its Manitou cave, a wonderful formation in the limestone rocks in the side of Lookout mountain. It was probably one of the natural fortresses of the Cherokee Indians, and from its rocks the Confederate government made saltpetre. It abounds in beautiful formations, subterranean rivers and cascades. A sur-

MANITOU CAVE. INTERIOR AND EXTERIOR VIEWS.

vey has been made for several miles by the company, bridges, stairs and railings built, and guides provided. When lighted, as it often is, by thousands of candles, it presents a sight never to be forgotten. Electric lights will be introduced and new wonders will doubtless be revealed. Around the entrance of the cave a beautiful park has been laid out, and it is a place of resort by visitors.

FORT PAYNE FIRE CLAY WORKS.

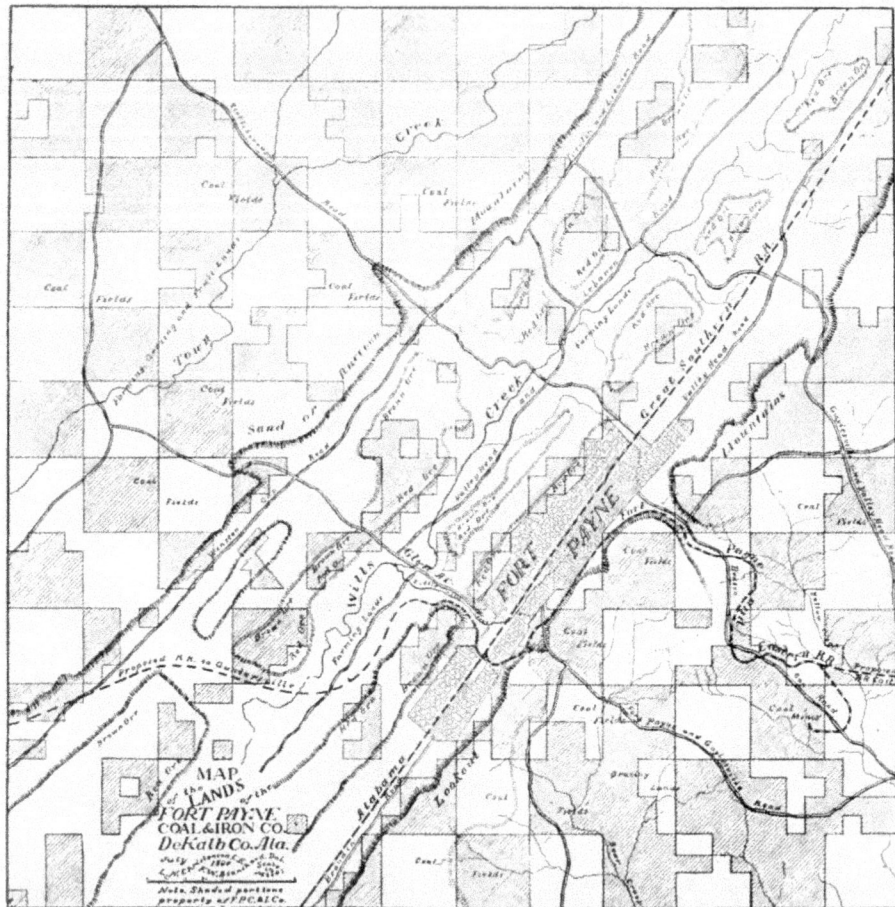

MAP
of the
LANDS
of the
FORT PAYNE
COAL & IRON CO.
DeKalb Co. Ala.

Note: Shaded portions
property of F.P.C.&I.Co.

Each of the squares on this map represents a section, one mile square, government survey. The shaded portions represent the property of the
Fort Payne Coal and Iron Company.

IRON

ORES, MINES, FURNACES, STEEL.

WEST of the City of Fort Payne, running parallel to the Lookout and Sand Mountain ranges, is a series of ridges from two hundred and fifty to three hundred feet in height, and well covered with forest trees. The ridge nearest the city, and upon whose slope Fort Payne is being built, is called Iron Mountain, from the great quantity of iron ore contained in it. The above-named ridges extend the whole length of the Wills Valley, being a section of a similar mineral belt extending from Birmingham on the south to Chattanooga, Tenn., on the north, and are practically one mass of iron ore, comprising the main ore deposit owned by the Company. The seams of the richest ore vary from three to thirty-two feet in thickness, and lie in parallel strata separated by beds of sandstone and the clayey soil, which is red in color owing to the presence of a large per cent. of oxide of iron, caused by the infiltration of water from the ore. An analysis of some of this soil has given as high as eleven per cent. of metallic iron.

The iron mines now being developed are located in Iron Mountain, west of the Fort Payne Furnace Company's plant, and east of the Bay State Furnace Company. On the east slope at a distance of about 800 feet from the Fort Payne Furnace Stock House

TRESTLE FROM BROWN ORE MINE, No. 1, TO FORT PAYNE FURNACE.

is opened and now operated the Brown Ore or Limonite mine. This has been fully developed by stripping and by drift into the face of the ore, and is known to extend in a southerly direction 1,500 feet before it goes beneath the surface. It also extends northerly to Mill Gap with a thickness at the drift of twenty-four feet of good ore. The indications show very plainly that this thickness will be increased from five to ten feet as it runs under the hill. A large body of this ore, enough to run the furnaces for years, can be used without washing. An analysis of the unwashed ore shows:

Silica, ... 20.02 per cent.
Metallic Iron, . 47.09 "
Phosphorus, . 0.28 "

This analysis represents the "run of mine" as it will be delivered to the furnace stock house. An incline is built by which the ore can be run directly into the stock house of the Fort Payne furnace, or loaded at the Fort Payne and Eastern Railroad on cars for market. As now developed the mine will have a capacity of 200 tons per day.

On the west side of Iron Mountain the red hematite ore has been fully developed to show five distinct veins of iron ore, varying in thickness at the outcrop from three to fourteen feet. The three foot veins of ore increase in thickness as the drift extends into the mountain, some of them now showing a thickness of seven feet. These veins lie above one another in a distance of 200 feet from the highest to the lowest, and are divided by sandstone and clay ranging from twenty-five to fifty feet in thickness.

The red hematite belongs geologically to the fossil iron ore, which is so called from the fact that the iron oxide appears in the shape of complete or fragmentary shells of marine animals, partly bivalves, partly snails, partly sea lilies or crinoids. An analysis of a sample of this ore obtained by boring through the thickness of the different veins shows: Silica, 4.11 per cent.; metallic iron, 25.39 per cent.; caustic lime, 30.13 per cent.; phosphorus, 0.336 per cent.

This ore, although low in iron, is really a valuable ore for the furnace, the high per cent. of caustic lime making it desirable for a flux for the soft hematite and limonite ores, thus reducing the amount of limestone to be added to the mixture in the furnace.

At the outcrop of the red hematite ores, where it has been exposed to the elements, it is known as the soft red ore, and when freshly mined can be easily cut with a carpenter's saw. This ore can be readily mined by stripping, and is of such good quality that it is economy to strip a foot of surface for every inch thick-

Glen Avenue Mine.

ness of ore, unless hard rock is encountered. An analysis of a sample of the soft red hematite ore, an average of all the vein as it will be delivered to the furnaces, shows: Silica, 10.37 per cent.; metallic iron, 55.34 per cent.; phosphorus, 0.46 per cent.; caustic lime, 1.07 per cent.

All of the ores on the east of Iron Mountain, including the red hematite veins and the soft ore, will be loaded into mine cars by chutes, thence run by gravity to the loading terminal of an incline, which will convey it to a discharging station on the line of the railroad. It will then be weighed and conveyed to its destination. The machinery of the different inclines will work automatically, the loaded cars in their descent pulling up the empties. As now planned the ore can be got out in a most economical manner, and can be taken from the mine and loaded on the cars without rehandling. The present capacity of the red ore mines is about 300 tons per day. The cost of getting out either the red or brown ore, when the mines are in working condition, will be 75 cents per ton. From the Mill gap, extending north from one and a half to two miles above the city, the same veins of brown and red ore have been traced and their quantity and quality fully developed.

Fort Payne Furnace.

The brown ore is found in larger quantities and same quality as that now worked, and the red ores, both hard and soft, are shown in their proper position, well defined and known to be the same as that which is now being mined

About 30,000 tons of the soft and hard ore have been exposed by stripping directly west of the centre of the city on Iron Mountain. It is proposed in the near future to open these mines with a view of supplying the market from Birmingham on the south to Chattanooga on the north. From the mines the ore will be conveyed to the top of the ridge, and thence down to a spur of the A. G. S. railroad by an endless wire rope haulage system, by which the ore will be loaded into iron buckets, passing over the mountain to a terminal discharging station at the railroad, and automatically weighed into the cars. This plant will have a capacity of 1,000 tons a day.

Besides the above mentioned fields, large bodies of iron ore have been located on the Sand Mountain range, including a man-

ganese ore or pyrolusite. This ore has been analyzed by Prof. Brainerd, of Birmingham, and shown to have 54 per cent. of manganese, a very rich ore, which could be shipped to Pennsylvania, or better still, could be smelted in the form of spiegeleisen or ferro-manganese. This ore in the future is destined to be a source of large income to the Company.

Deposits of red and brown ore have been also located on Lookout range, but being found in such abundance on Iron Mountain, they have not yet been given much attention by the mining engineer.

The articles on coal and iron have been prepared by Col. J. H. Mullin, mining engineer.

FORT PAYNE STOVE WORKS.

Manufacture of Iron.

Iron ores as they come from the miners' cars consist of different forms of oxide of iron, (metallic iron combined with different portions of oxygen), and also foreign matter, silica (in the form of sand and clay), phosphorus, sulphur, etc. Much of the clay and sand is removed from the ore by washing, but a certain portion passes through the furnace and is finally removed by the action of heat and the different gases resulting from the combustion of the fuel and limestone. The operation of reducing the iron ores to metallic iron in the blast furnace is strictly a chemical one, a chemist's assay carried on on a grand scale, using masses of ore and flux measured by the hundred pounds instead of a few grams. The operation, however, is one of accuracy, nothing being left to chance, but following the chemist's analysis the proportion of every part of the material put into the furnace (the "burden") is calculated, the proper amount of air necessary to produce the required amount of heat is known; therefore, with a well designed furnace, managed by a skillful founder and using good ores, it is easy to produce any grade of iron required by the market.

The blast furnace having been properly "dried out," or freed from all moisture contained in the brick work, is filled up inside with fuel. A short scaffold of lumber is first built, cord wood then piled in "on end" until it reaches nearly to the "bosh"; coke is then added and fire applied to the bottom. After the whole mass is well lighted, light charges of ore, coke and limestone are added, sometimes furnace cinder is used, and after six or eight hours the blast is gently "turned on" and the gas passes through the down-comer and gas flues to the boilers and stoves, furnishing heat for steam and hot blast. In the meantime the proper charge of ore, coke and limestone have been put in the furnace until it is filled within, say, twelve feet of the top.

The action of the gases and the combustion of the fuel and the reduction of the limestone to caustic lime, have removed the oxygen from the oxides of iron, converting it to metallic iron. The carbon from the fuel and the silica from the ore have furnished the required amount of carbon and silicon; the result is cast-iron. The interior of the blast furnace has been divided into three zones. Commencing at the top is the zone of preparation, from thence to about half way from the bosh to tuyeres is called the zone of reduction, and thence to a point just above the tuyeres is the zone of fusion. In about two hours after charging into the furnace the ore commences to lose its oxygen at not quite red heat. The first signs of metallic iron are seen in about six hours, when the mass is red hot. In half an hour more than fifty per cent. of the oxygen is removed at a temperature sufficient to soften wrought iron, and a complete reduction will occur in about nine hours, when the mass of metal is ready to pass into the crucible of the furnace.

From the top of the furnace down to the tuyere the walls slightly widen, to allow the contents to pass downward as rapidly as possible, but from the bosh the walls approach each other, forming a funnel-shaped shaft, which compresses the mass of melted ore and limestone, forming an arch above the tuyeres, and the great weight of material above presses this together, and, like a huge sponge, the contents are "squeezed" out and drop, a fiery rain of molten iron and cinder, to the bottom. The slag, or cinder, being lighter, floats on top of the iron, and protects it from the oxidizing influence of the heated air.

This continued rain of iron and cinder gradually fills the crucible of the furnace, and as fast as cinder reaches a certain height, the cinder notch is opened and the slag is blown out. This is done as often as necessary, and when the melted iron has accumulated in sufficient quantity the iron notch is tapped and the iron is run out and cast into pigs. The process of filling a blast furnace is continuous throughout the twenty-four hours. A cast is made from three to four times in twenty-four hours.

The Fort Payne Furnace Company.

The Fort Payne Furnace Company was organized on the 27th of April, 1889, with a capital of $200,000. The directors are: W. P. Rice, J. M. Ford, J. W. Spaulding, C. O. Godfrey, S. C. Hathaway, H. B. Peirce and H. B. Hill. J. M. Ford is president; C. O. Godfrey, vice-president; S. C. Hathaway Jr., secretary and treasurer, and John H. Mullin, superintendent. Ground was broken for the construction of the foundations May 24, 1889. The foundations were put in by Fred. Wagner. The iron work, including pumps and engines, by Alex. K. Rarig & Co., of Columbus, O., and all the brick work by John McGarry & Co.

This furnace is located on Gault avenue, one mile south of the DeKalb hotel, on the main line of the Fort Payne and Eastern railroad. The property consists of ten acres of land and is a very desirable site. The stack is 65 by 14 feet, which is small compared to most southern furnaces, but was selected by the superin-

FORT PAYNE ROLLING MILL.

tendent because it is better adapted to the ores of the district than larger sizes. The nominal daily capacity is 75 tons. The blast is heated by three Siemens-Cowper fire brick stoves, each 65 by 16 feet. The cast house is brick, 110 by 45 feet, with corrugated iron roof. The stock house is frame, iron roof and sides, 150 by 75 feet, with two tracks fifteen feet high. An iron hoist tower, with a Crane vertical hoist, takes the stock to the tunnel head. The

engine house is brick, 55 by 35 feet. It has two blast engines, each 72 by 48 by 36 steam cylinder. The steam is supplied by eight boilers, each 52 inches by 28 feet, with two 18-inch flues. The draft stack is iron, 170 feet high, and 8 feet 6 inches in diameter in the clear. There are two Gordon supply pumps, 15 by 18 inches, and two boiler feed pumps, 9 by 16 inches. An 8 inch artesian well supplies pure water to the boilers and furnace.

This furnace is very eligibly located for its supply of raw materials, and the owners believe that pig iron can be made in it at a less cost than at any other locality.

The Bay State Furnace Company.

The Bay State Furnace Company was organized on April 19th, 1890, with a capital of $250,000. The directors are C. O. Godfrey, H. B. Hill, J. W. Spaulding, A. W. Train and S. Reed Allen, all of Fort Payne, Adna Brown, Springfield, Vt.; A. E. Hemphill, Holyoke, Mass.; J. L. H. Cobb, Lewiston, Me., and R. P. Kingman, Brockton, Mass. The officers are President, C. O. Godfrey; vice-president and general manager, H. B. Hill; treasurer, H. B.

GENERAL VIEW OF IRON MOUNTAIN LOOKING EAST FROM GARRETT FARM.

Hill; secretary, True P. Pierce. Ground was broken for the construction of the foundation April 27, 1890, and the contract awarded to John McGarry & Co. The iron work was contracted for by Messrs. Alex. K. Rarig & Co., of Columbus, Ohio, builders of the Fort Payne furnace. The Bay State furnace is located 3,500 feet west of the Fort Payne furnace, on Little Wills creek, and near the Glen Avenue boulevard. The property consists of fifteen acres of land, and is very desirably located on account of water, and for dumping cinder slag. This land gives ample room for two more furnaces when desired, and the reservoir, constructed at a slight cost, is a great point in favor of this location, water for furnace purposes in some cities costing from $4,000 to $5,000 per year. The reservoir is a natural formation, which if dammed slightly at one end, would contain three to four millions of gallons of water, and is only 100 feet from the furnace. Lying close to the foot of Iron Mountain, ore can be put into the stock house by chutes from the great vein; ore, coke and limestone being delivered to either furnace at the same price.

The Company have erected a large boarding house and sufficient dwellings to accommodate their employees. The furnace lies on the line of the Fort Payne and Eastern railroad, between the Sand Mountain coal fields and Iron Mountain, and has a full and complete system of tracks. The capacity of it will be about 75 tons per day.

The maps of the Fort Payne Coal and Iron Company's property and the city of Fort Payne were prepared from official sources by Messrs. Christensen and Blanchard, civil engineers, and the railroad map was made by W. T. Carley and J. W. Bailey, railroad engineers, all of the Fort Payne Coal and Iron Company.

Steel.

The business of the Fort Payne Rolling Mill is the manufacture of soft steel from the pig iron, smelted in the furnaces at Fort Payne. This pig iron, as it is well known, contains from three-quarters to one and one-quarter per cent. of phosphorus, which it is necessary to remove from the metal in order to obtain from the steel converting furnaces a merchantable article. This result is obtained by melting the pig iron in an open hearth regenerative furnace, substantially the same as is used in all the different countries of the world where steel is manufactured. The process for removing the phosphorus from the metal consists simply in lining the melting chamber of the furnace with magnesia, and the use of raw limestone to absorb the phosphorus. This material is imported from Europe in two forms—one of which is a brick, which is made under heavy pressure after the magnesia has been calcined, and the other is in a loose state as it comes from the calcining furnaces. The bricks are used to form the melting chamber, and the loose material to repair the chamber from time to time. This material has been in use in Europe since 1858, and is now extensively used in the United States; furnaces lined with this material often running a year without repair. It is now an established fact that soft steel, or ingot iron, manufactured by this process is the softest and most ductile steel now offered in the markets of the world. Tests of this steel have been made, showing a tensile strength, reduction of area and elastic limit fully up to the United States government requirements, viz.: Tensile strength, 58,000 pounds; elongation 34 per cent; reduction of area, 54 per cent. This steel was made from a low grade of mottled iron purchased from different furnaces in Alabama. The analysis of this steel averages: Carbon, .07; phosphorus, .02, showing the phosphorus to be practically eliminated from the metal.

The Fort Payne Rolling Mill will soon be ready to supply in any quantity, steel of above quality, to manufacturers requiring the best grades. The plant consists of two 15-ton open hearth furnaces, one 32-inch, two high reversible blooming mills, one 22-inch nail plate train, capable of rolling plates 15 inch wide, down to No. 21 guage; one 16-inch bar mill, and one 9-inch guide mill.

The plant is so arranged that the pig iron can be converted into steel, and carried through the rolls and made into merchantable bars and plates without loss of heat. In conjunction with the mill the company have arranged to put into operation a number of self-feeding nail machines, by which they will work up into nails a great portion of material which, by its size, would have to be remelted. The establishment of this mill has resulted in the location of a number of iron-working plants in Fort Payne, and all kinds of stamped iron, wire goods, hardware, steel rails, etc., can be made from its productions. The officers of this company are C. O. Godfrey, president; A. W. Train, vice-president and general manager; H. R. Godfrey, secretary and treasurer; all of Fort Payne.

Limestone.

Limestone is found in abundance on the Lookout range of mountains in two stratas, locally known as the upper and lower limestone veins. They are both shown on the face of the mountain. The upper limestone strata is from 75 to 100 feet thick, extending from Beeson's Gap to several miles below the city; and the lower strata crops out at the foot of the mountain and extends north beyond the limits of the town. These limestones are of excellent quality, suitable for furnace flux, easily quarried, and can be delivered at the furnace stock house at thirty-five cents per ton. On the east side of Red Ridge or Iron Mountain, closely connected with the red ores, limestone appears in abundance and excellent quality. It can be easily quarried and is sufficient in quantity to supply all the furnaces which will be built here for many years to come.

MINES, COKE AND OVENS.

THE coke which is used for fuel to convert the ores into pig iron is made from a seam of coking coal locally known as the Castle Rock Seam. It is opened on Lookout Mountain and shows a thickness of thirty to sixty inches. The Lookout mine, opened during the past year by driving entries, is well ventilated, has good drainage and dry roadways; and the coke ovens, in full operation, will have a capacity of 200 tons a day, which may be increased at pleasure. At the Lookout mine, which is situated on the Fort Payne and Eastern Railroad, a village has been built with houses for operatives. A school house, church, store and post office have been established, and a telephone connects the store with the Company's office in the city.

to Town creek, and it is proposed in the near future to open these fields by a shaft or shafts, and establish a large coke plant of 1,000 ovens and a mining center. The locality, topography and mineral resources of this mountain seem to warrant the belief that here we have a second Connellsville.

On Lookout a large area of unbroken coal field can be worked from the present openings. Adjoining this tract is another section of unbroken coal, as shown by prospecting with the diamond drill in several places. This field can be mined advantageously by shafts located near the line of the Fort Payne and Eastern Railroad, at a point most favorably situated for a mining town and a coking plant. North of this point to Beeson's Gap, is a continuous field

GENERAL VIEW OF SAND MOUNTAIN—LOOKING WEST.

On Sand Mountain this same seam of coal has been opened in six different places, showing the same quality, from 30 to 44 inches in thickness. An area of about fifteen square miles of coal can be reached on Sand Mountain, extending from the bluff east

of coking coal, which is cut out at the ravine making the gap. Crossing this the coal opens the same in quality, but thickening up to about five feet.

A second seam of coal lying above this is here distinctly defined showing from 24 to 37 inches. This same seam has been opened opposite the city (Edgemont mine), and shows 37 inches, underlying a bed of fire-clay eight feet in thickness. This coal and clay are advantageously situated for mining in an economical manner, the output being conveyed by an incline to the Fort Payne and Eastern railroad, about 1,000 feet below.

Coke.

Coke is the carbonaceous residue produced when the coal is subjected to a strong heat, out of contact with the air, until the volatile constituents are driven off. It consists essentially of carbon, (the so-called fixed carbon), together with the incombustible matters or ash contained in the coal from which it is derived. In addition to these it almost invariably contains small quantities of hydrogen, oxygen and nitrogen, the whole, however, not exceeding two or three per cent. It also contains water, the amount of which may vary considerably according to the method of manufacture. When produced at a low heat, as in gas making, it is of a dull black color, of a loose spongy or pumice-like texture, and ignites with comparative ease, though less readily than bituminous coal, so that it may be burnt in open fire places ; but when a long continued heat is

LOOKOUT (MINING) VILLAGE.

used, as in the preparation of coke for iron and steel melting, the product is hard and dense, and is often prismatic in structure, has a brilliant semi-metallic lustre and silvery grey color, is a good conductor of heat and electricity, and can only be burned in furnaces provided with a strong chimney draught or an artificial blast. The strength and cohesive properties are also intimately related to the nature and composition of the coals employed, which are said to be coking or non-coking, according to the compact or fragmentary character of the coke produced. The simplest method of coking, that in open heaps or piles, is conducted in a very similar manner to charcoal burning. The coal is piled in a domed heap about thirty feet in diameter and five feet high, with a chimney of bricks arranged in open chequer work in the centre, around which the largest lumps of coal are placed, so as to allow a free draught through the mass. The outside of the heap is covered with a coating of wet coke dust, except a ring about a foot high at the bottom. Fire is communicated by putting a few live coals near the top of the chimney, or from the interior by throwing them down the chimney, and the combustion proceeds downward and outward by the draught through the uncovered

LOOKOUT COAL MINES—LOOKOUT MOUNTAIN.

portion at the bottom. Whenever the fire takes too strong a hold and burns out to the surface it is damped by plastering over the spot with wet coke dust and earth, this being a point requiring considerable skill on the part of the coke burner. When flame and smoke are no longer driven off, which usually happens from five to six days, the whole surface is smothered with coke dust, and the chimney is stopped for three or four days longer, when the heap is sufficiently cooled to allow the coke to be broken up and removed, or as it is called, "drawn." The cooling is usually expedited by throwing water upon the heap before drawing. The principle of coking in rectangular pile is generally similar to the foregoing, but chimneys are not used. The dimensions generally adopted are a height of from $3\frac{1}{2}$ to 5 feet, and a breadth of 12 feet at the base.

Coke Ovens at Fort Payne Furnace.

The oldest form and simplest form of "clamp" or "kiln" for coking coal is the bee-hive oven, consisting of a round chamber about eleven feet in diameter, with a cylindrical wall and domed roof rising about six and one-half feet above the floor. A hole about one foot in diameter in the crown of the roof serves for charging, and the finished coke is drawn through a door in the wall about two and one-half feet square. When cleared for a

fresh charge, the oven being red hot, small coal is introduced through the hole on the roof, and spread uniformly over the floor until it is filled up to a level of the springing of the roof, when the doorway is filled with loose bricks, which give a sufficient passage between them for admission of air to ignite the gases given off by the distillation of the heated coal. After a few hours these airways must be closed by plastering up the brickwork, except the top layer, which is left open for twenty-four hours. The heat developed by the burning gases causes the coking to proceed downward until the entire charge is converted, this taking from forty-eight to seventy-two hours, according to the quantity of the coal. When the escape of flame from the hole in the roof ceases, all apertures are stopped whereby air can enter to the incandescent mass, which being no longer protected by an atmosphere of combustible gases, would burn to waste if brought in contact with the atmosphere. At this point all holes in the oven and chimney are entirely closed for about twelve hours, when the door is opened, and the coke,

FORT PAYNE EXHIBITION BUILDING.

coke, as compared with that of the original, may be roughly stated at about one-half. The Fort Payne Coal and Iron Company have erected a plant of one hundred bee-hive ovens of improved construction, and are now manufacturing the coke used by the Fort Payne Furnace Company. They have a capacity of about 200 tons per day. The plant includes complete machinery for crushing and washing the coal, and handles it at the lowest possible cost. The coal as it comes from the mine is dropped into the "run of mine" coal bin from the cars, conveyed to the crushers, consisting of a lump breaker and fine rolls, which crush the coal to a uniform size, about ¼ inch

which forms a coherent mass, somewhat less in size than the original charge and divided by a system of columnar joints, is removed by hooks and scrapers; water from a hose being used to quench the glowing coke as it is brought out. In some cases the cooling of the coke is effected by watering before drawing. A certain amount of sulphur is removed by this method, as the steam generated, being brought into contact with the sulphide of iron in the heated mass, formed from pyrites in the coal, produces sulphuretted hydrogen and magnetic oxide of iron. The amount of desulphurization by this method is, however, practically insignificant, as the operation does not last long enough to permit the mass of fuel to be affected. The proportion of sulphur in finished

cubes. After passing through the crushers, it is conveyed by elevator to the washers, where a large portion of the slate and ash, producing material is removed. Then it is elevated to the washed coal bin, loaded into a "larry" and conveyed to the coke ovens. When converted into coke it is loaded into the furnace-charging buggies and without rehandling conveyed to the furnace hoist. From the ovens coke is loaded into cars for other furnaces and the market. Other ovens will soon be constructed. An analysis of the coke made from the Company's coal shows: moisture, 0.15; volatile gases, 0.64; fixed carbon, 91.67; sulphur, 1.1182; ash, 6.42. It is a dense bright looking coke with a metallic ring, comparing very favorably with that from the Connellsville district.

Fire Clays, Building Stone, Timber, &c.

I N the rapid and extensive development of the iron and steel industries of Alabama, one of the essentials is a refractory material in the form of fire-bricks used in the construction of the numerous blast furnaces, rolling mills, etc., for which, up to the present time, Pennsylvania and Ohio have been the base of supply. In the prospecting and development of the Fort Payne mineral field, numerous and valuable deposits of fire-clays, flint, etc., have been opened up, analyzed and tested in the furnace; and so satisfactory were the results, and so assured was the Fort Payne Company that they had material to make into fire brick suitable for the southern furnaces, that they erected and equipped one of the largest and most modern fire clay works in the country, which is now completed and in full operation.

The Beeson Gap fire clay mine is on the company's property,

ROCKY GAP. B.. WILLS VALLEY.

immediately adjoining their mineral railroad. The vein varies in thickness from six to eight feet of good clear fire-clay; this is overlaid by a roof of coal which is afterwards taken down and utilized. Another vein of fire-clay is now being opened up in the immediate locality, with promising results. For the manufacture of a very refractory fire brick a proportion of flint, which is infusible, is added. A deposit of this flint has been opened out and connected by rail with the works. Prof. Brainerd's analysis of this flint gives silica, 98.454. It is quite white, a portion of it being in a decomposed state, and is proved to a depth of over twenty feet. This flint may well be classed as one of the precious materials mentioned in the prospectus of 1889.

Another bed of plastic fire-clay is being worked near the fire-clay works. This, used in connection with the Beeson Gap fire-clay, is being manufactured into vitrified salt glazed sewer pipe in all sizes up to twenty-four inches diameter. The combination of these two fire-clays produces sewer pipe possessing the desired dark glaze and a body thoroughly vitrified. Its suitability for this manufacture may be better expressed when it is stated that sewer pipe of similar quality cannot be procured nearer than St. Louis or Ohio.

From these fire-clays separately, and blended together, architectural terra cotta is now being made in various natural colors, and it is intended that Fort Payne shall be the headquarters for architectural terra cotta in the Southern States. Skilled artisans are now employed in producing the same, and, judging from specimens of the work, this cannot fail to be one of the growing industries of Fort Payne.

Among the many mineral deposits around Fort Payne classed as fire-clays, the richest, and one promising the most satisfactory results, is the kaolin or china clay, a body of which from two to three miles in length has been secured, the thickness of the vein being upwards of forty feet, and practically inexhaustible. The kaolin or china clay, with the halloyosite contained in the same, has for some years been extensively mined and shipped to the china factories at Trenton, N. J., and East Liverpool, Ohio, and there manufactured. Ware made from this material has recently been sent to the Company's offices, and the manufacturer of this ware said it was whiter and clearer than any American or English on the market; that while the material was made up for china the product was semi-porcelain or bisque. There are millions of tons of this in reserve, and interested parties have in contemplation to at once erect an extensive pottery and commence the manufacture of china and porcelain ware for the Southern States, now entirely supplied by northern potteries. The numerous deposits of fire-clays, flint, kaolin and terra cotta clays, so excellent and suitable for manufacture, alone should build up Fort Payne, independent of its other mineral resources.

Limestone abounds in great quantities and is used in kilns and by the Southern Paving Company. Sandstone of excellent color has been used with excellent effect in public and private buildings. A new quarry of a high grade pink and light red sandstone has been opened on Lookout Mountain near the Fort Payne and Eastern Railroad, and developes an immense quantity of easily quarried stone.

The various woods found on the Coal and Iron Company's property on Lookout and Sand Mountains comprise various oaks, including Spanish, red, white and water oaks, hickory, poplar and black gum, and in some sections ash and pine are found. These woods are now used by mills in Fort Payne, and in the future other wood-working plants will utilize them for making furniture, etc.

The following by Prof. A. F. Brainerd, analytical chemist and assayer for the Fort Payne Coal and Iron Company, speaks for itself:

BIRMINGHAM, Ala., July 26, 1890.

Fort Payne Coal and Iron Company:

GENTLEMEN—In selecting samples of iron ore, limestone and coal for analysis, when I have had the opportunity to select for myself, care was taken to get a great number of small specimens, rather than a single large one, of the different stratas, so as to get a fair average sample. Since the Fort Payne Coal and Iron Company, or its predecessors first prospected and opened up their property, in developing their mineral wealth, the quality of the two red iron ores (the "soft fossil ore" containing no carbonate of lime, and the "hard fossil ore" where the carbonate of lime predominates) has not changed much, as they were good from the start. The hard ore especially, which has silica ranging from 4½ per cent. to 6½ per cent., which is much lower than any ore of this variety in this or adjoining States. The size of the veins of the "hard ore" has increased from two and a half feet to eight feet a few thousand feet from where it was first opened up.

The "brown ore" was discovered from surface specimens, and was at first thought to be of limited quantity, but upon prospecting and digging into it, the whole side of the mountain just back of and near to the Fort Payne furnace, was covered with it to the depth of several feet in thickness, with but light "stripping" near the middle and along the sides and of excellent quality. The coal has improved very materially and is now from 60 to 70 per cent. lower in ash than when first opened up. Hence the volatile matter, and particularly the fixed carbon, has increased proportionally. The limestone ledges have shown good from the start and it is a first-rate "stone" for "furnace flux," or any other purpose. I have never seen any mineral property show up any better nor, of equal prospects, increase so rapidly in quality or in quantity, or of such uniform continuity of stratas, with so few geological faults or disturbed rocks. Everything is in its proper place and uniform quality. Respectfully yours,

ALFRED F. BRAINERD,
Analytical Chemist and Mining Engineer.

CITY AND FARM PROPERTY.

. . . .

THE following description refers to various sections of the city in which the Fort Payne and Iron Company have property for sale for residences, business, or for manufacturing purposes.

NORTHERN EXTENSION—Begins one-half of a mile from the centre (coal and iron building) and runs northward seven blocks. This is a fine residence and business quarter. Lots vary from 25 by 110, to 50 by 150. It is but one-quarter of a mile from the new railway station.

GREEN ADDITION—Lies 1,000 feet east of the Builders' Hardware Company, at the foot of Lookout Mountain, on high rolling ground. This is a good location for tenements. Lots 50 by 120.

FOREST ADDITION—This property lies on the slope of Iron mountain, from one-quarter to one-half of a mile from the centre,

and is elevated from 50 to 150 feet above Gault avenue. This is the favorite residence portion of the city, and is now being built up with handsome houses. Lots vary from 50 by 150 to 75 by 190 feet. It is covered with forest trees, has city water, electric lights, etc.

HIGHLAND ADDITION—Lies one-quarter of a mile west of the Court House. This is a fine residence quarter, and lies on Iron Mountain overlooking the city, being from 75 to 150 feet above Gault avenue. Lots run 50 to 75 feet front by 120 to 175 feet in depth.

CAVE ADDITION—Lies east of the A. G. S. R. R. at the foot of Lookout Mountain, on high rolling ground, and within five minutes walk of brick kilns, fire-clay works, stove works, foundry and pavement works. Lots 50 by 117½. It is a first-class location for tenements, and has water, electric lights, etc.

GLEN AVENUE BOULEVARD.

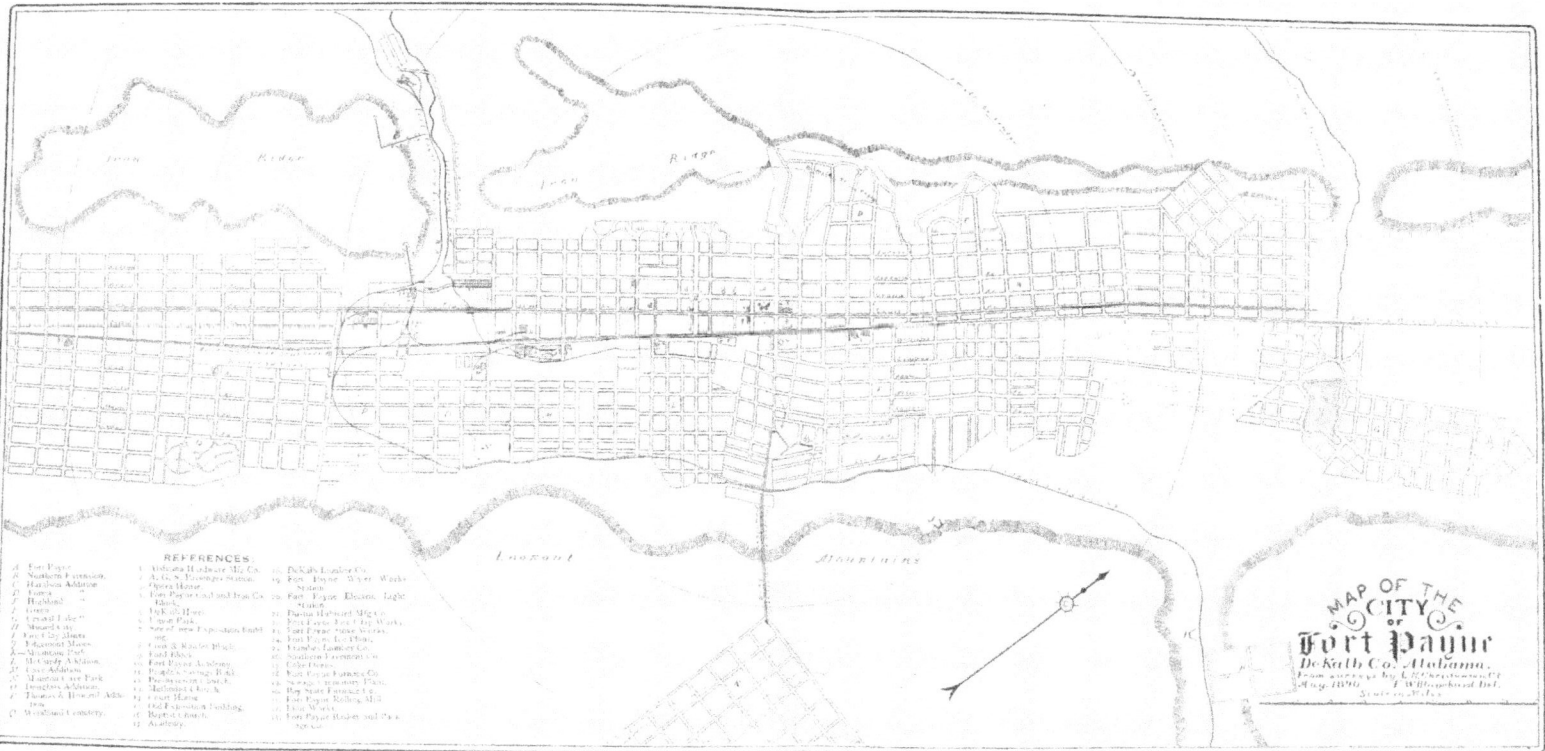

MAP OF THE
CITY
OF
Fort Payne
DeKalb Co. Alabama.
From surveys by L. K. Christianson C.E.
May 1890.
F. W. Blancheland Del.
Scale in Feet

REFERENCES:

A   Fort Payne
B   Northern Extension
C   Hudson Addition
D   Kemp
E   Highland
F   Green
G   Grand Lake
H   Mozart city
I   Ford City Mants
K   Edgemont Manor
L   Mountain Park
M   McCurdy Addition
N   Crow Addition
O   Martin's new Park
P   Douglass Addition
Q   Thomas J. Howard Addition
R   Woodland Cemetery

1   Alabama Hardware Mfg. Co.
2   A.G.S. Passenger Station
3   Opera House
4   Fort Payne Coal and Iron Co. Block
5   DeKalb Hotel
6   Court Park
7   Site of new Exposition Bldg.
8   Cox & Rhodes Block
9   Bank Block
10 Fort Payne Academy
11 Peoples Savings Bank
12 Presbyterian Church
13 Methodist Church
14 Court House
15 Old Exposition Building
16 Baptist Church
17 Academy

18 DeKalb Lumber Co.
19 Fort Payne Water Works Station
20 Fort Payne Electric Light Station
21 Payne Hardwood Mfg. Co.
22 Fort Payne Tool Chip Works
23 Fort Payne Stone Works
24 Fort Payne Ice Plant
25 Lumber Lumber Co.
26 Southern Foundry Co.
27 Coke Ovens
28 Fort Payne Furnace Co.
29 Savage Laundry Plant
30 Bay State Furnace Co.
31 Fort Payne Rolling Mill
32 Iron Works
33 Fort Payne Basket and Case

McCURDY ADDITION—One eighth of a mile north of the Cave Addition, on high rolling ground, good residence lots, 50x100 feet.

HARALSON ADDITION—This property lies immediately north of the Forest Addition along the slope of Iron Mountain and is covered with trees. This is the location of the proposed grand hotel, and the view of the valley is very fine. It is three-quarters of a mile from the centre. Lots 50x125 feet and 75x150 feet.

FORT PAYNE.—The section of the city designated on the map of the city as Fort Payne, is that section of the city which includes the original village site, and lies west of the A. G. S. R. R., extending from the

THOMAS AND HOWARD ADDITION—Lies one-quarter mile east of the rolling mill and furnace on F. P. & E. R. R. It is on high rolling ground. Lots are 50x150 feet, suitable for tenement houses.

DOUGLASS ADDITION—Lies near the southern portion of the city, and has been reserved for the colored population. Lots are 40x117½ in size.

MOUND CITY—lies on the brow of Lookout Mountain, on the line of the Fort Payne and Eastern Railroad, and about three miles from the city. It is near the fire-clay and coal mines at Beeson's Gap. A tract of forty acres has been laid out with streets, and lots are 150x200 feet. The Coal and Iron Co. have in both the Big and

School House, Douglass Addition.

Fort Payne furnace on the south to within one mile of Crystal Lake on the north, and is bounded west by Forest avenue, including also a section of land east of the railroad, now partly occupied by manufactories. The southern part is devoted to manufactories, the central part to business, and the northern part to residence sites. The Company offers special inducements to investors.

Little Wills Valleys good farming lands, and also farm property on Lookout and Sand Mountains. Wherever these lands have been cultivated they have yielded good returns to the farmer. They are located near to the railroads, and are of easy access to the city and a good market for farm products. Applications to the office of the Company will receive prompt attention.

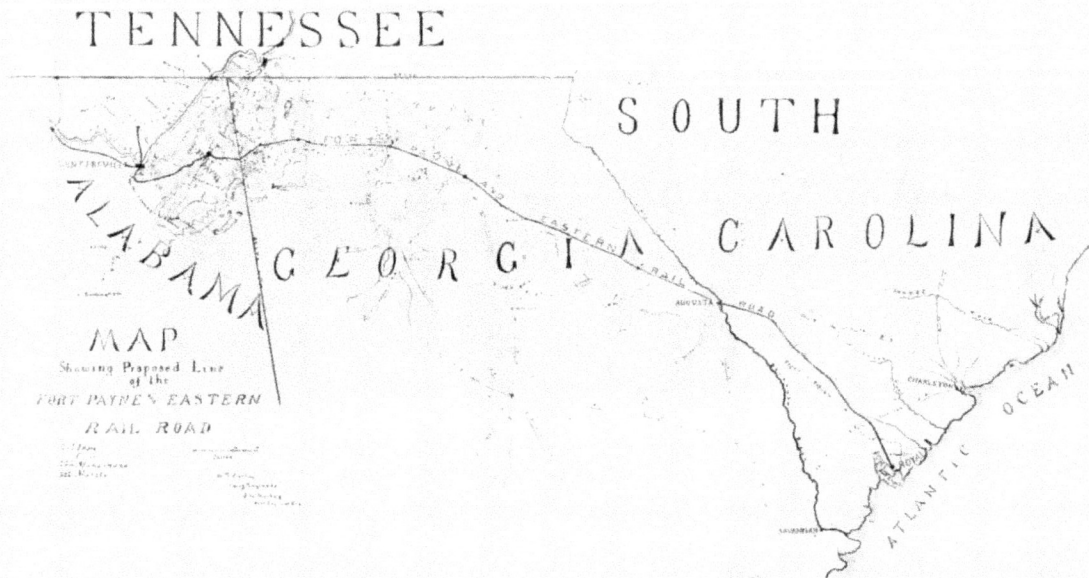

TENNESSEE

SOUTH

ALABAMA

GEORGIA   CAROLINA

MAP
Showing Proposed Line
of the
FORT PAYNE EASTERN
RAIL ROAD

ATLANTIC OCEAN

Fort Payne and Eastern Railroad.

The Mineral Railroad now in operation was built and is now owned by the Fort Payne Coal and Iron Company. It is designed to form a link in a through east and west line to connect the Tennessee River with the Atlantic coast. It has been named and called by the Company the Fort Payne and Eastern Railroad. The charter in the state of Alabama, however, is called the Guntersville, Fort Payne and Chattooga Valley Railroad. An organization has been perfected under that charter with the following officers: W. P. Rice, president; J. W. Spaulding, vice-president; C. O. Godfrey, general manager; F. H. Tobey, cashier, and the following directors: W. P. Rice, J. W. Spaulding, C. O. Godfrey, J. M. Ford, F. H. Tobey, Wm. Warner, L. A. Dobbs, E. E. Parker, H. C. Young. Another charter crosses the state of Georgia, and is in the name of the Fort Payne and Eastern Railroad Company. Both charters were granted in 1889.

Pumping Station and Springs of the Fort Payne Water Works.

THE CITY OF FORT PAYNE.

THE city of Fort Payne was chartered by act of the legislature of Alabama February 28, 1889, and the first municipal election for mayor and councilmen was held July 1, 1889. The following officers were elected: Mayor, C. O. Godfrey; aldermen, A. W. Train, J. J. Nix, W. H. H. Minot, A. F. Payne and S. E. Dobbs.

Under the charter thus obtained ordinances were passed for the government of the city, including laws against the sale of liquor. A police department was organized, sanitary inspection, street opening, grading, sewerage, etc., were provided for. The city was bonded December 2, 1889, for the following purposes: Sewerage, $35,000; streets, $10,000, and city building, $10,000.

A complete system of sewerage, under competent engineers, is now in progress, which includes a deodorizing cistern and a cre-

mating furnace. It is the policy of the city to proceed as fast as possible to open and grade streets and avenues, thirteen miles of which were graded by July, 1890, and to extend the water and street light system as rapidly as possible.

The products of the Southern Pavement Company, whose plant is in the city, will enable the council to pave streets in the near future at a minimum of cost with asphalt blocks. Many difficulties in the topography of the city have been overcome, and as fast as streets are located they are built upon, often before they can be graded. Care

GAULT AVENUE AT UNION PARK.

has been taken to provide parks and drives, and Gault avenue, the main business street and driving avenue, which runs the entire length of the city and into the adjacent country, and the Glen avenue boulevard, are as fine streets as any in the United States. The class of dwellings built in the city are fully equal to any city of the North, as a few examples pictured in this book will show. Gault avenue has some fine business blocks, and a large number are under contract at present.

The taxable property in Fort Payne in 1888 was $146,633 ; in

The health of the city since its foundation has been excellent. In spite of the discomforts and exposures incident to the founding of a new town, deaths have been very few, either among new settlers or in the old village.

DeKalb Hotel.

1889, $1,189,268, and in 1890, $3,000,000. The rate of taxation is fixed by state law for the city and county and is one-half of one per cent. for each.

The census figures for 1890 are not yet available, but will not show less than 3,575 people, and if taken in the fall of 1890 it would show nearer 7,000, owing to the influx of operatives.

There are three church edifices in the city, Methodist, (South), Cumberland Presbyterian, and Baptist. A Congregational society will be formed in the coming fall, (1890), and a Methodist church, (North), and an Episcopal church are organized and worship in halls. Early in 1889 a Young Men's Christian Association was organized, and handsome rooms, with magazines and papers, are open every evening, and religious meetings are held weekly. The colored people have churches in various parts of the city.

The secret societies are Masonic, Odd Fellows, Knights of Pythias, and a post of the G. A. R., which includes many loyal mountaineers.

There is one large private school and several district schools, including a colored school in the Douglass Addition. Measures are being taken to establish a high grade school, which is to be the nucleus of technical schools and eventually a university. A system of public schools will be provided for the city, which will be managed on a liberal scale.

Numbers of new and elegant private residences will be open for social festivities in a few months, and the coming winter will inaugurate the home life of the citizens of Fort Payne as never before, and the abodes of culture and refinement will add a new charm to the city.

The temperature of the Wills Valley during the hottest season, on account of the altitude, is always endurable, and the nights are cool. From the fact that scores of Northern-born men stayed the entire year of 1889, most of the time out of doors, with none of the comforts now enjoyed, is a proof that the Southern highlands is a salubrious place to live in. On the mountain top, immediately opposite the city, preparations are being made to establish a summer resort, where the thermometer is always ten degrees below the temperature of the valley. An incline road will make access easy.

The birdseye view pictured in this book is an accurate sketch of the city and its various buildings. It is taken from Lookout Mountain, and many dwellings on its slope cannot be shown. The limits of the old village are indicated in the sketch, and the wonderful growth of the city can be seen by comparison. Not a half dozen houses were outside of the village in March, 1889, which is now included in four blocks of the present city.

A street railway company has been organized, and will operate a road on Gault avenue in 1890, and eventually on Godfrey and Alabama avenues. This road will be in operation in October, 1890, and will run from the rolling mill on the south to Crystal lake on the north, a distance of five miles.

FORT PAYNE AND EASTERN RAILROAD TRAIN.

The city water has force enough to throw streams of water over any building in the city, and hose and reels are provided for fire purposes.

Mineral Railroad.

The Mineral Railroad, a division of the Fort Payne and Eastern Railroad, was built by the Coal and Iron Company, under the direction of Chief Engineer W. T. Carley, in order to bring the coal from the mines, and to facilitate business in the city, by extending tracks to all of the furnaces, mills, etc. The road is eleven and a quarter miles long, with two miles of sidings, laid with sixty-pound steel rails, standard guage, well ballasted with stone and constructed in the best possible manner. The road runs from the A. G. S. R. R., in the valley, up and along the side of Lookout Mountain northerly to Beeson's Gap, thence easterly to its present terminus at Lookout (coal) mine. The sidings ramify all over the manufacturing district, connecting the works with the main line, and allowing freight, etc., to be unloaded at the doors of the factories. It has been a most important factor in building the city. The equipment consists of 5 locomotive, combination passenger and baggage coach, coal and construction cars, etc. Regular trains run from the city to Lookout Village,

The Fort Payne Educational Association.

The Fort Payne Educational Association was organized June 24, 1890, having for its object the establishment of a system of schools of high grade, to be operated as preparatory schools for a university, to be founded in the city of Fort Payne in the near future. The Fort Payne Academy for Young Ladies is the first school of this system, and commences its work October 1, 1890. The principal has associated with him a corps of competent teachers, selected with special reference to their adaptation for the duties of the departments they are to fill. Two regular courses have been provided—college preparatory and academic. The first is specially adapted for students who desire to enter college, and is in-

FORT PAYNE ACADEMY.

stopping at convenient points, and already does a considerable passenger and freight traffic with the public, outside of the business of the Company and the great mills and furnaces. The road was commenced November 4, 1889, and completed January 20, 1890. The main line will ultimately be absorbed in the Fort Payne and Eastern, described on another page. The Mineral Railroad division of the Fort Payne and Eastern will shortly be extended through the Great Wills Valley to Sand Mountain, where great iron mines and coal fields will be developed and coke ovens placed.

tended to prepare for matriculation in colleges of highest grade. The second is largely elective, including ancient and modern languages, literature, sciences, music and art. A student may elect three studies for each semester, with the approval of parent or guardian. Each course covers a period of four years.

It has been decided to open in connection with the academy a grammar school for the accommodation of day pupils from the city, and in order to meet the demand which is felt in all schools of high standing, for supplementing work which has been imperfectly done. The importance of this department cannot be over-estimated, for here the foundation of a thorough education is laid. This department gives an opportunity for the pupil to pursue the regular course, and at the same time make up the study or studies in which she may be deficient. Special advantages are afforded in music and art. A daily record of standing will be kept, and a monthly report forwarded to the parents. At the close of each semester there will be written examinations.

A course of lectures on popular subjects will be given during the winter months by the best talent that can be secured. Students will also be permitted to attend such lectures and entertainments in the city as may be approved by the principal, provided they do not hinder the progress of the pupil or interfere with the regular work of the school.

Particular attention will be given to home culture, both as to manners and morals; and appropriate home lectures will be delivered, from time to time, bearing upon such topics as may seem to be helpful in shaping character and developing those qualities of heart and mind which are essential to true culture. Proper care will also be given to the development of the physical constitution. Classes in calisthenics under the direction of an experienced teacher will be formed, and each student will be required to take regular exercise every day.

The academy is to be in no sense sectarian, but thoroughly Christian in all its teachings and its methods. Students will be required to attend chapel service every morning and at least one service in the city on Sabbath. Each student may attend the church of her choice, but when the choice is made at the beginning of the year no change will be permitted without the consent of the principal. The academy is situated on a rise of ground at the base of Lookout Mountain, which here towers nearly eight hundred feet above the valley. It commands a fine view of the city and of the charming Wills Valley for miles above and below. The building is new and elegantly furnished, supplied with steam heat, electric light, and all the comforts of home. The school rooms are large and well ventilated, and provided with all modern conveniences.

RESIDENCE OF W. P. RICE, ESQ.

The success of the enterprise is assured by the enthusiasm with which the citizens have taken hold of their first school. It is expected that next year a military academy for boys and young men will be erected on the top of Lookout Mountain, just above the ladies' academy. It is also the purpose of the Educational Association to have the university ready as soon as the first class in the preparatory schools shall have completed the preparatory course.

DeKalb Co.

DeKalb county, of which Fort Payne is the county seat, lies in the extreme northeastern part of Alabama, and is bounded by Georgia on the east, the northern end touching the line of Tennessee.

proper cultivation, will yield bountiful crops. "Apples, pears and peaches, and indeed all fruits grown in this latitude, attain perfection. No section in America can display finer specimens of plums than those grown in this region."—(Riley's Alabama Guide). The crop of cotton for 1890 promises to be the finest for many years, and will probably exceed 12,000 bales. The peculiar quality of DeKalb county cotton has given it a reputation among cotton buyers.

The commissioners of DeKalb county have authorized the erection of a court house to cost $40,000. The plans of the architects have been accepted, and the building will be built immediately. New iron bridges

RESIDENCE OF HON. C. O. GODFREY.

The total area is 740 square miles, and the population is between 15,000 and 18,000. Two great plateaus occupy most of the county, Sand or Raccoon, and Lookout Mountains. These two great plateaus are separated by the Great and Little Wills Valleys, which cut across the county from northeast to southwest. The agricultural lands can be divided into the stiff dark soils of the valleys and the lighter soils of the plateaus, each of which, under

have been ordered to span various streams, and the roads are being improved in all directions. The establishment of the city of Fort Payne has appreciated the price of property all over the county, and when the projected line of railroad penetrates the county to the southern end, the farming area will be greatly increased and the population doubled in a few years. The mineral resources of the county constitutes its greatest wealth, but the agricultural value of the valleys and plateaus when properly developed will add greatly to the aggregate value of this region.

"DeKalb County, Alabama, shows the largest increase of any county in the State in assessed valuation, as far as heard from. The assessed valuation of property in the county is $5,200,201, which is an increase over last year of $2,208,009. Fort Payne did it."—*Evening News, Chattanooga.*

The Fort Payne Commercial Club.

An organization for the advancement of the business and social interests of the City of Fort Payne has been formed, and will immediately arrange for temporary club rooms, so as to be ready to entertain those who may come to the city as visitors and prospectors.

Elegant rooms will probably be secured on Gault avenue, opposite the DeKalb hotel, in the very centre of the city, in a building which is now being erected, where the Club will permanently arrange suitable quarters, to include parlors, reception rooms, billard, reading and smoking rooms, bowling alleys, etc.

The effect of a first-class club cannot fail to be beneficial to the city, and will soon constitute a powerful body of men whose influence on the city at large will be felt at all times.

A place for the reception of distinguished visitors has been needed for some time past, and the Commercial Club will be prepared to receive and entertain individuals and parties from abroad, as is the custom in other cities. The office of the club in

RESIDENCE OF TRUE P. PIERCE, ESQ.

helping on the interests of the city, will be like that of a Board of Trade or Chamber of Commerce, where questions of importance can be discussed, and movements made which shall be for the good of the entire community.

The formation of this club is another evidence of the steady progress of Fort Payne on the line of providing means for social enjoyment, and for the promotion of the varied manufacturing, business and educational interests of the city, and its work cannot fail to tell in the future.

It is hoped that when the readers of this book shall have looked at the pictures and read the statements therein contained, that they will some time come in person (if they have not already visited the "Electric City") and see for themselves what has been done in building up a city, not merely in furnaces and great mills, but in many other things that relate to the moral, social and intellectual status of a community. Much remains to be done, but much has already been accomplished, and the work of less than two years has often taken in older communities many years to work out to a successful solution.

On the 8th of September the fires of the Fort Payne Furnace were lighted, and some hours later the first draft of iron was made. This elaborate plant, a description of which can be found on another page, has all the modern appliances for making iron, and went into blast without any of the trouble incident to a new furnace. The quality of the first iron made was much superior to that expected, and various combinations of ores are being made which produce as fine grades of iron as any furnace in the South.

RESIDENCE OF A. C. SPAULDING, ESQ.

On the 30th of August, 1890, Hon. D. H. Goodell, First Vice-President of the Fort Payne Coal and Iron Company, resigned

RESIDENCE OF F. J. MITCHELL, ESQ.

his office on account of ill-health, and Hon. W. P. Rice was elected in his place. Mr. Rice is now devoting his ener-

gies in directing and promoting the interests of Fort Payne. The birdseye view of the City of Fort Payne, which has been

RESIDENCE OF W. H. H. MINOT, ESQ.

drawn by a special artist, was taken from the side of Lookout Mountain, looking west over the city. Care has been taken to

RESIDENCE OF F. H. KENNEDY, ESQ.

represent the city just as it appears to the spectator; no contemplated buildings having been inserted. It shows the natural advantages of the place as the site for a great manufacturing city, and gives a clear idea of the location of the various industries

RESIDENCE OF GEORGE H. MERRIMAN, ESQ.

already established with their convenient proximity to the iron and coal mines and other mineral deposits, and their connection with the markets of the country by the railroads. The distance

to the Basket Factory, on the extreme left of the picture, is necessarily shortened, and there remains in this direction, as well as in

RESIDENCE OF O. S. POWERS, ESQ.

other parts of the city, abundant room for many other manufacturing industries. The residences of the city are mainly in the northern part and on the slopes of the surrounding hills.

RESIDENCE OF JAMES M. VERNON, ESQ.

BANK · OF · FORT · PAYNE

Organized March 1, 1889, with a Capital of $50,000, Increased July, 1890, to $100,000.

W. P. RICE, President.
J. M. FORD, Vice-President.
F. H. TOBEY, Cashier.

DIRECTORS,

W. P. RICE,
J. M. FORD,
J. W. SPAULDING,

J. D. RAWLES,
C. O. GODFREY,
L. A. DOBE,

L. L. COCHRAN,
F. H. TOBEY,

DIVIDENDS, MARCH AND JULY, 1890, 10 PER CENT.

First National Bank of Fort Payne.

ORGANIZED AUGUST 1, 1889. CAPITAL, $50,000. SURPLUS, $1,500.

W. P. RICE, President. GEO. E. LATHROP, Cashier.

A. W. TRAIN, Vice-President. E. P. LANDERS, Ass't Cashier.

DIRECTORS,

W. P. RICE.   E. B. COOK.

G. E. LATHROP, C. O. GODFREY.

A. W. TRAIN.

DIVIDENDS, 4 PER CENT., JANUARY AND JULY, 1890.

PEOPLE'S SAVINGS BANK.

INCORPORATED
UNDER LAWS OF
ALABAMA,
JUNE 21, 1890.

CAPITAL.
$50,000.

SAFE DEPOSIT VAULT.

The People's Savings Bank will add a Safe Deposit business, and are erecting a large steel vault. The vault is composed of "Brooklyn chrome steel and iron," fastened with heavy steel plugs and counter-sunk machine screws, making a secure burglar-proof structure. The vault is secured by a day door inside of heavy double doors, with combination lock and massive outer door, weighing four tons. The total weight of the vestibule and inner doors is six and a half tons. The vault contains five hundred safes of various sizes, which will be rented by the year. No safe can be opened without the "master key" in the hands of the bank and the key of the holder.

FORT PAYNE INVESTMENT CO.

A Corporation, Organized June 23, 1889.   *Capital, $140,550.*

This Company was incorporated for the purpose of managing, in a methodical and judicious manner, large land interests. The Company owns in fee nearly 1,700 acres of land, consisting of city lots and improved acreage property located in various parts of the City of Fort Payne, and in the County of DeKalb, immediately adjacent to the city. Quite a portion of the land has been platted and is on sale. A small fractional part of the land owned by the Company has been disposed of, and the proceeds divided to the stockholders, the contributors having already received 75 per cent. on their investment. The very large amount of land still remaining, and its desirable location, assure the stockholders several hundred per cent. ultimate profits on their investment.

President, W. P. RICE.   *Vice-President,* J. W. SPAULDING.   *Secretary and Treasurer,* TRUE P. PIERCE.

DIRECTORS:

W. P. RICE,	HORATIO ADAMS,	F. A. TOBEY,
J. W. SPAULDING,	C. O. GODFREY,	TRUE P. PIERCE.

THE · SOUTHERN · BANKING · COMPANY.

Chartered March, 1889.   Capital Stock, $100,000.

The Company is chartered to do a general banking business and is empowered " To buy, improve, lease or sell lands; to build, lease, rent or otherwise use buildings or land of any description; to issue bonds not exceeding the amount of real estate held by it; to issue bills, notes, mortgages and securities; to guarantee indebtedness to persons and corporations; to deal in stocks as trustee, or to take stock in any other corporation."

The Banking Company investigates titles, and will make reports on the value of any mineral or timber land in Northern Alabama, Georgia or Tennessee, and if thoroughly satisfactory to them, advise their purchase, and not otherwise.

The Southern Banking Company, through its correspondents in the Northern States and in Europe, can render valuable assistance to owners of Southern properties.

C. O. GODFREY, *President,* A. W. TRAIN, *Vice-President,* E. DUDLEY FREEMAN, *Secretary,* TRUE P. PIERCE, *Attorney.*

Directors—C. O. GODFREY, A. W. TRAIN, E. DUDLEY FREEMAN, TRUE P. PIERCE, J. W. SPAULDING, SELDEN CONNOR, HORATIO ADAMS.

The York Syndicate

(INVESTMENT COMPANY.)

INCORPORATED UNDER THE LAWS OF ALABAMA, AUGUST, 1890. WILL GIVE ESPECIAL ATTENTION AS INVESTORS' AGENTS FOR ALL SECTIONS OF THE SOUTH, AND TO ATTAIN THAT PURPOSE RESPECTFULLY SOLICIT CORRESPONDENCE. ADDRESS

S. F. SHAW, Pres't, Biddeford, Me.   · J. H. HATCH, Treas., Fort Payne, Ala.

RICE INVESTMENT COMPANY

FORT PAYNE, ALABAMA.

W. P. RICE, President.
GEO. E. SMALLEY, Treasurer.   *Capital $250,000*

Transacts a General Loan and Investment Business   Buys and Negotiates Commercial Paper, City, Town, County and State Bonds.   Negotiates Long and Short Time Loans.   Pays 6 per cent. interest on 6 months; 7 per cent. on 9 months, and 8 per cent. on 12 months or longer time deposits.

C. D. REAMER, ... Real Estate Broker,

GAULT AVENUE, FORT PAYNE.

Specials for Large Syndicates.   Fine Gold Property, Silver and Lead Mines. Marble Lands and Select Town Sites, Coal, Ore and Timber Lands, City and Suburban Property, Residence and Business Property. Rentals and Collections attended to,   Correspondence solicited.

. . . . THE DE KALB COUNTY ABSTRACT COMPANY . . . .

OF FORT PAYNE, ALABAMA,

For the Investigation of Land Titles.   An Abstract of Title to any Land or Lot in DeKalb County, Ala.   Complete Abstract Books.

EUGENE THOMAS, Attorney.   CHAS. M. SAWYER, Manager.

J. A. WILDER,

REAL ESTATE AND INVESTMENT,

Correspondence Solicited.

OFFICE, FIRST NATIONAL BANK BUILDING.

ABBOTT & PEAKES,

Insurance · Agents

Represent the Leading Fire Insurance Companies of the United States.   OFFICE: No. 4 COOK & RAWLE'S BUILDING, GAULT AVE.

E. B. COOK. J. D. RAWLES. GEORGE UNIACKE.

FORT · PAYNE · HARDWARE · COMPANY.

Dealers in General and Builders' Hardware, Carpenters' Tools, Mining Supplies, Stoves, Tinware, Paints, Oils, Varnishes, Brushes, Etc. Agents for the Celebrated Atlas Ready Mixed Paints.

The Alabama Builders' Hardware Manufacturing Co.

[As . the . name . implies, . will Manufacture . an . Extensive Line . of . all . grades . of

BUILDERS' HARDWARE,

from . the . most . elaborate Designs . in

BRONZE METAL

to . the . cheaper . grades . of Iron . Goods, . with . home . market . for . most . of . the . product. The . outlook . is . one of . the . brightest, . and . it . is looked . upon . as . one . which will . bring . with . it . its . own reward, . inasmuch . as . the line . of . goods . produced . will be . of . such . a . nature . that it . will . require . a . high . and

intelligent . class . of . operatives . to . produce . the . desired . results; . hence . in . the . establishment . of . this industry . we . are . assured . that . the . citizens . of . Fort . Payne . will . be . proud . to . class . its . employees . as among . her . best . citizens.

E. B. COOK, *Vice-President & Treas.*   E. S. STEVENS, *Secretary.*

DUSTIN-HUBBARD MANUFACTURING CO.,
ENGINEERS, FOUNDERS AND MACHINISTS.

Machinists' Tools, Steam Engines, Cotton Machinery, and General Machine Work,
LOCATED ON ANDERSON STREET AND THE A. G. S. R. R.

The Machine Shop is 40 x 160 feet, and 40 x 40 feet, two stories; Foundry, 50 x 100 feet; Engine and Boiler House, 40 x 60 feet; Pattern Shop, 40 x 100 feet two stories; Pattern House, 30 x 60 feet. A boiler-making and sheet-iron shop will be erected in connection with the plant. The works are already engaged in casting and making machinery for various plants in the city, and will do a very extensive business with the city and surrounding country during the coming winter.

SOUTHERN PAVEMENT COMPANY
OF
Fort Payne, Alabama.

HENRY B. PEIRCE, *President.*

CHAS. H. GIFFORD, *Treasurer.*

The Southern Pavement Company is organized under the laws of Alabama, has a capital of $60,000—six hundred shares of $100 each—and has obtained from the International Pavement Company of Baltimore, Maryland, the exclusive right to manufacture and sell compressed Asphalt Block and Tile Pavement in East Tennessee, nearly all of Georgia, and in all of Alabama and Mississippi. The quality of this pavement, which renders it specially desirable for residence streets, may be briefly stated thus:

1. It is comparatively smooth without being inherently slippery, nor does it polish from use, as is the case with stone blocks.

2. It is comparatively noiseless, giving forth but little sound from the striking of the iron shoes of horses, or the rolling of wheels upon it—a most desirable quality for residence street pavement.

3. It is sanitary in the highest degree; the blocks are non-absorbent, and being uniform are laid close together, and the joints, which are filled with fine clean sand, are soon practically closed by compression from traffic, thus preventing the absorption of noxious liquids.

4. It is durable when laid on a gravel and sand foundation. It has stood well for as long as seven or eight years under a very heavy traffic, and it will remain in good order without repair at least ten years, and in streets where the traffic is light it will last for twenty years. And if laid on a cement concrete foundation it will greatly increase the tenure of durability.

The dimensions of the blocks are 12 by 4 by 5 inches, weighing about 21 pounds each.

The dimensions of the tiles are 8 by 8 by 2½ inches, weighing about 14 pounds each. They are also made hexagonal in form.

Capacity of the plant 6,000 blocks per day of ten hours. Blocks made from our limestone have greater durability than any yet made by this process, which is duly protected by patents in the United States, Canada, Great Britain, France and other countries.

Blocks produced by this mechanism have been in use in Baltimore, Philadelphia, Washington and in other cities many years, and have given complete satisfaction.

Correspondence from all points in the South relative to public or private work is invited.

RAILWAY PASSENGER DEPOT,
FORT PAYNE, ALA.,
ALABAMA GREAT SOUTHERN RAILROAD.
Chas. C. Taylor, Architect, Cincinnati, O.

THE FRAMBES LUMBER CO.

The grounds and buildings occupy about four acres, and are located on

NINTH ST. AND THE A. G. S. R. R.

About 75 men are employed. They are Wholesale and Retail Dealers in Lumber and Mill Work, Manufacturers of Sash, Doors and Blinds, Mouldings, Turning and Scroll Work, &c. Ornamental and Carved Work, Interior Fittings for Banks, Public Buildings and Dwellings, in standard and fancy woods a specialty. Dry kiln capacity 10,000 feet per day.

FORT PAYNE Basket and Package FACTORY.

Situate at the southern end of the city on the line of the A. G. S. R. R. The grounds and buildings cover 3½ acres. Local woods are used exclusively for making Splint Baskets, Butter Dishes, Crates, Spokes, Axe and other Handles, Thin Veneers, &c. The factory employs 150 hands, and is extending its trade every day.

E. G. GOODPASTURE,
General Manager.

CRYSTAL LAKE LAND CO.

TWO MILES FROM THE CENTRE OF THE CITY.

• • • • • • • • • • •

A BEAUTIFUL suburban property, in the northern part of the city, delightfully situated in a picturesque locality, near to the city and yet far enough away to be free from many of the annoyances attending a residence in a manufacturing town. The property contains 442 acres of land, 400 acres of which have been platted into building lots, 50x130 feet, upon which will be placed many very fine villas. The great attraction will be the Crystal Lake, a beautiful sheet of water covering 15 acres. Lookout Mountain rises at the foot of the lake to the east, and its wooded heights are pictured on the surface of the water. Parks and avenues have been laid out, leading from the A. G. S. Railroad to the lake, and everything that art can do, to assist nature, will be done in making the property a delightful place to live winter and summer.

Crystal Lake is readily accessible by driving, and will soon be reached by the street railway in fifteen minutes. A hotel and refreshment saloon for parties driving out to the lake, and for boating parties, will be erected next season.

As a point for investment no locality near the city offers such a chance, as it will be the most desirable place of residence at or near Fort Payne. Away from the manufacturing centre, with all the advantages of a country residence, yet near enough to churches, stores, etc. Fine residence lots are now on the market at reduced prices. The first buyers are certain to realize handsome profits. Prices according to location.

J. W. WILLARD, *President.*   E. W. GODFREY, *First Vice-President.*   J. N. SHAPLEY, *Second Vice-President.*

C. M. IDE, *Secretary and Treasurer.*   F. E. DONAHUE, *General Manager.*

OFFICE:

HOUGHTON BUILDING, OPP. COAL & IRON CO.'S BUILDING.